MONUMENTAL MILESTONES
GREAT EVENTS OF MODERN TIMES

Hurricane Katrina
and the Devastation of New Orleans, 2005

The streets of New Orleans were heavily flooded from Hurricane Katrina.

Mitchell Lane
PUBLISHERS

P.O. Box 196
Hockessin, Delaware 19707

Titles in the Series

MONUMENTAL MILESTONES
GREAT EVENTS OF MODERN TIMES

Hurricane Katrina
and the Devastation
of New Orleans,
2005

The flooding was so extensive that people had to get around in boats.

John A. Torres

Mitchell Lane PUBLISHERS

Copyright © 2006 by Mitchell Lane Publishers, Inc. All rights reserved. No part of this book may be reproduced without written permission from the publisher. Printed and bound in the United States of America.

Printing   1   2   3   4   5   6   7   8   9

Library of Congress Cataloging-in-Publication Data
Torres, John Albert.
    Hurricane Katrina and the devastation of New Orleans, 2005 / by John A. Torres
        p. cm. — (Monumental milestones)
    Includes bibliographical references and index.
    ISBN 1-58415-473-X (library bound : alk. paper)
    1. Hurricane Katrina, 2005—Juvenile literature. 2. Disaster victims—Louisiana—New Orleans—Juvenile literature. 3. Disaster relief—Louisiana—New Orleans—Juvenile literature. 4. Rescue work—Louisiana—New Orleans—Juvenile literature.
I. Title II. Series.
HV551.4.N43T67 2006
976.3'35064—dc22   2005036804

ISBN-10: 1-58415-473-X   ISBN-13: 978-1-58415-473-0

ABOUT THE AUTHOR: John A. Torres is an award-winning journalist covering social issues for *Florida Today*. John has also written more than 25 books for various publishers on a variety of topics, including *P. Diddy*, *Clay Aiken*, *Mia Hamm*, and *Disaster in the Indian Ocean, Tsunami, 2004* for Mitchell Lane Publishers. In his spare time, John likes playing sports, going to theme parks, and fishing with his children, stepchildren, and wife, Jennifer.

PHOTO CREDITS: Cover—Kyle Niemi/Getty Images; p. 1—James Nielsen/AFP/Getty Images; pp. 3, 9—Mario Tama/Getty Images; pp. 6, 30, 38, 47—John Torres; p. 11—Dave Einsel/Getty Images; p. 14—NOAA/Sharon Beck; p. 18—Sharon Beck; p. 22—Mark Wilson/Getty Images; p. 26—Eric Gay/AP Photo; p. 27—David J. Phillip, Pool/AP Photo; pp. 28, 36—Army Military.

AUTHOR'S NOTE: See p. 47.

PUBLISHER'S NOTE: This story is based on the author's extensive research, including his personal trip to New Orleans in September 2005, during which he witnessed the devastation firsthand and spoke to dozens of survivors for this book.

The internet sites referenced herein were active as of the publication date. Due to the fleeting nature of some web sites, we cannot guarantee they will all be active when you are reading this book.

PLB

Contents

Hurricane Katrina and the Devastation of New Orleans

John A. Torres

*For Your Information

Tena Corley stops to talk with reporters in an evacuated New Orleans just days after Katrina destroyed her home.

All of Corley's personal belongings are in the shopping cart, which she and her husband, William, pushed around New Orleans. They made sure they had plenty of clean water to drink.

CHAPTER 1

Honeymoon in New Orleans

William and Tena Corley were married four days before stories of a strong hurricane heading for New Orleans became a serious concern.

They heard about it on the news, but like most people, they didn't really take notice until the storm had grown to mammoth proportions and was only a day or two away.

The Corleys were poor. Because they were originally from other parts of the country—he was from Los Angeles and she was from Texas—they decided to spend their honeymoon in their newly adopted city, "The Big Easy," New Orleans. They had lived there for only about six months and had moved into an apartment together. They didn't have a lot of money to take an expensive honeymoon trip anyway.

When the storm was approaching, many of their neighbors had decided to leave the city. In fact, by the time the storm neared, Tena and William were the only ones left in their small apartment building. William had survived a few earthquakes in California, so he didn't worry much. He thought a hurricane was just a little wind and rain. It couldn't be as bad as an earthquake. He was wrong.

William had another motive for wanting to stay around during the storm. He figured there would be plenty of work available for him in the construction field to rebuild the area once the storm blew over.

Just a year earlier, he had seen what the four hurricanes that hit Florida had done for the construction industry. Work crews—some from out of state—were kept busy for all of 2005 rebuilding houses and patching damaged roofs.

Hurricane Katrina picked up speed and intensity as it neared New Orleans. Sustained winds were being measured at a catastrophic 160 miles per hour.

At first, the Corleys thought it was a little romantic. After all, here they were in a famous city that was pretty much empty because many of the residents had evacuated. The howling wind moving through the city's streets sounded beautiful.

"It was just a big wind blowing and sheets of water coming across the city," William Corley said. "It was kind of nice."[1]

But the nice, romantic feelings would soon fade as the fierce storm began to grow stronger. The Corleys were only experiencing the fringes of the gigantic hurricane, which by this time had sucked up warm waters from the Gulf of Mexico and gained even more strength.

Hurricane Katrina had grown into a monster storm. It was changing between a category 4 and category 5 on the Saffir-Simpson Hurricane Scale. The weakest type of hurricane is a category 1 storm. That means the winds blow at between 74 and 95 miles per hour. A category 5 hurricane is the strongest type of storm. In addition to pulsing rains, a category 5 has sustained winds of more than 155 miles per hour.

Saffir-Simpson Hurricane Scale

Category	Wind Speeds	Damage
1	74–95 mph	Minimal
2	96–110 mph	Moderate
3	111–130 mph	Extensive
4	131–155 mph	Extreme
5	over 155 mph	Catastrophic

The hurricane had missed Florida, but it looked like it was headed directly toward the Louisiana and Mississippi coasts. It was traveling slowly but seemed to be getting stronger every hour. The local government ordered the people of certain cities to leave. New Orleans was one of those cities. The problem for many of the area's poor people—including William and Tena Corley—was that they could not really afford to go.

The city of New Orleans set up temporary emergency shelters at the Superdome—where the New Orleans Saints play football—and the city's Civic Center. Even before the storm hit, there were rumors that there wouldn't be

enough food or security at the shelters. People were afraid the buildings wouldn't hold up.

The Corleys were among the few who decided to wait out the storm in their home. And to be honest, they didn't think it would be too bad. They thought it would just be more comfortable to be inside their own place.

When William and Tena Corley heard the rain tapping against their window, they had no idea of the wrath that was about to descend on the area.

A little while later, Tena recalled, the storm got scarier.

"The winds got a little stronger and things, you know objects, started hitting the building," she said. "We started to feel a little afraid when things began to hit our windows. We thought they would break."[2]

A few very long hours later, it was morning. The storm was still in full force. The wind was howling and sending stray objects flying through the city streets. The Corleys wanted to see what the conditions outside were like, so

Inside the Superdome, tired and hungry New Orleans residents wait for relief.

Thousands of the city's residents sought refuge in the Superdome, where the New Orleans Saints football team normally plays. Unfortunately, the supplies quickly ran out, and the building began leaking from the storm.

they walked down the stairs of their second-floor apartment to the front door of the building.

When William Corley opened the door, his eyes widened in utter amazement as water started rushing into the building. For a split second he was shocked, not knowing what to do. He struggled to close the door, but the water and the howling winds made it difficult. Once it was shut, he and Tena ran upstairs to their apartment and bolted the door. He yelled to his wife to get to an inner room.

They took food, water, and a battery-operated radio into the bathroom—they had supplies for a few days if needed. William Corley wasn't sure if the rising waters would reach the second floor. After a few hours the winds quieted down and the storm seemed to have finally passed. But was it safe? What would their newly adopted city look like?

The couple emerged from their hiding place and ran to the nearest window. They were relieved that the water had not crept up into their apartment.

They took in the scene outside. Trees were strewn everywhere. Branches and utility poles were scattered like fallen leaves. The water and the wind had moved parked cars into the middle of the street. The worst of the storm had passed, but clearly it was not gone for good. Every few minutes, strong winds and driving rain would start up again for short periods.

"I looked out the window and the water was hip-high,"[3] William Corley said. He expected that the waters would soon subside and that their lives would return to normal. He looked forward to helping out in the reconstruction efforts.

By mid-afternoon the water level had not dropped at all. In fact, the water was rising! The hurricane had caused the waters of the Gulf of Mexico to surge forward onto the shore in a way that was eerily similar to how the Asian tsunami of 2004 had driven the Indian Ocean ashore. The difference was that this water surge was happening slowly. The city's water pumps—used to pump water back out into retention ponds and rivers in times of flooding—had stopped working.

Also during this time, some of the levees burst. The levees—a series of dams—had been built to protect the city of New Orleans from flooding by Lake Pontchartrain and the Mississippi River. They were built so that New Orleans, which is situated below sea level, could be used as a harbor city. The

U.S. Army Corps of Engineers started building them along the Mississippi River in the late 1800s—but they were never intended to withstand a category 4 or 5 hurricane. Newer levees were built after a hurricane in 1947 flooded Jefferson Parish—which includes New Orleans—but they would not be strong enough for a major storm. Weather experts predicted that the storm surge from Katrina could reach 28 feet high. Many of the 350 miles of levees around New Orleans were only 18 feet high.

Hurricane Katrina, combined with the aging levee system, was a disaster waiting to happen. When the levees failed, millions and millions of gallons of water rushed into the city's streets. With more rain falling and the storm surge still causing flooding, the water had nowhere else to go. The city's roads, from the back alleys to the main thoroughfares, became rivers. Houses, stores, offices, banks, and schools were flooded.

"The next morning the water was seven feet high," William Corley said. "We were afraid, but I guess God was on our side."[4]

Hurricane Katrina hit New Orleans hard. But it wasn't until the levees broke that the real damage started. Water escaped into the city, flooding property, killing hundreds, and forcing thousands of people to flee their homes.

When the levees broke, thousands of gallons of water rushed into the city of New Orleans.

The Corleys were lucky. They lived. But they knew that they had to get out of their apartment. They were pinned in, and soon vermin, like rats, snakes, and alligators, might be swimming in the streets and entering people's homes. They decided they would have to get out of that house. Their only choice was to swim for safety.

When the storm was finally over, they went downstairs and trudged and then swam away from their home to higher land. They found themselves in a city that offered them no services, no companionship, and no help. They were alone.

Eventually the water caused extensive damage to their home. The Corleys had not owned much, but whatever they had was gone. Five days after the storm was over, they were walking around New Orleans with a shopping cart full of bottled water, a cell phone, and the clothes on their backs. They were tired and hungry. William called out to the soldiers who had come to help and thanked them.

They still had no idea if their friends and family were safe. They didn't know—like most of America—how many people this killer hurricane had claimed. But they did know they had no place to go in New Orleans. They knew it would take months or years before the city would ever get back to normal.

"Nobody can believe that this was how we spent our honeymoon." Tena Corley smiled, though it looked like she wanted to cry. "It makes me laugh."[5]

She hugged her husband and they started walking down a street, pushing their cart. They said they would leave the state and go to Texas, where Tena's mother lives.

The Corleys had no idea that this storm would also cause tensions to escalate between federal and local governments, and between the nation's white and black communities. There was much disagreement over how the relief efforts were handled, and many believed that race had something to do with the nation's response time.

It would be a tough test for a country that had experienced the civil rights movement less than forty years earlier.

FYInfo

FOR YOUR INFORMATION

Mardi Gras. Cool jazz music playing on hot nights. Centuries-old French- and Spanish-style homes and buildings. Spicy Cajun gumbo. Alligators roaming the swamps. And zydeco music pulling together influences of American, French, and Caribbean music. These are some of the things that made New Orleans special—and then Hurricane Katrina caused levees to burst and the city to flood.

New Orleans has always been one of the most interesting and diverse places in the United States. Hopefully, once it is rebuilt, the Big Easy will once again reclaim the charm and character that has long made it a popular tourist destination.

To understand what makes New Orleans so unique, one must understand a little of the history of the mid–United States, from the present state of Louisiana north into Canada. This area, which came to be known as the Louisiana Purchase, was once a French Royal colony. It was claimed for King Louis XIV in 1699. In 1762, France gave most of the area to Spain, which gave it back in 1800.

Many French settlers called Louisiana and especially New Orleans home during the eighteenth century, and many stayed after the property was purchased by the United States in 1803. Many Spaniards also settled there, and many African slaves were brought in from the Spanish-speaking Caribbean. Eventually these three cultures—and many more—would blend to create a rich city filled with foods, lifestyles, and music different from anywhere else in the world.

History in New Orleans is important to the people who live there. In fact, New Orleans had roughly 40,000 buildings listed on the National Register of Historic Places—more than any other city in the country.

Louis Armstrong

Decades after New Orleans became a "French City in America," it became the birthplace for a type of music that combined Negro spirituals, European folk songs, and freewheeling musical expression. This music was known as jazz, and it was made famous by such legendary musicians as Louis Armstrong, Buddy Bolden, and Jelly Roll Morton. They all got their start in New Orleans nightclubs between 1897 and 1917. Jazz became a New Orleans staple, with such famous musicians as Harry Connick Jr. and Branford Marsalis calling the city home.

Over the years, the city has grown commercially as well, with the port in New Orleans creating business and commerce. The city even has its own professional basketball team, the Hornets, and a football team, the Saints. While moving ahead as a modern city, New Orleans has maintained its history and charm.

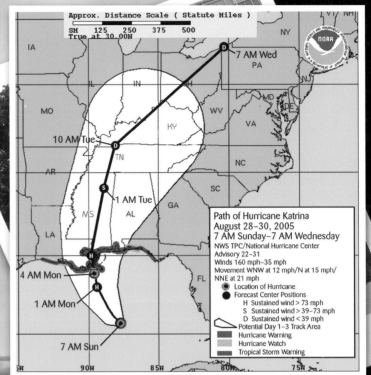

Hurricane Katrina made landfall at 6:00 A.M. on Monday, August 29, 2005. The thick black line indicates the path it followed before it hit land, and then afterward as it slowed to a tropical storm.

The storm came ashore in Buras, Louisiana, within 15 miles of the forecasters' predictions. It pounded the Gulf Coast with wind speeds as high as 160 miles per hour.

Suprise Storm

Normally the National Hurricane Center is able to track storms a few weeks away from making landfall near the United States. But Hurricane Katrina was different right from the start.

In the early morning hours of August 23, the hurricane center discovered a violent weather pattern forming very quickly just south of the Bahamas. Two days later the storm was strong enough to earn a hurricane name. Even though it had missed Florida's mainland, it still swatted the southernmost tip—the Florida Keys—and claimed 11 lives.

People asked, "Where did this thing come from?"

Some hurricanes lose steam once some landfall is made, but again, Katrina was different. After the Florida Keys, the storm gained strength in the Gulf of Mexico and started on a steady, direct path toward New Orleans.

The morning after Katrina hit Florida, Louisiana Governor Kathleen Blanco issued a state of emergency for her entire state. Governments will issue states of emergency before a catastrophe happens in order to mobilize the National Guard and other emergency personnel who may be needed. Weather reports said that the hurricane had become a category 2 and could develop into a major hurricane in another day.

"We are in the strike zone," the governor said.[1]

By Saturday, August 27, the National Hurricane Center announced that Katrina had become a "major hurricane" with sustained winds of at least 115 miles per hour. That evening, New Orleans Mayor Ray Nagin issued a voluntary evacuation of New Orleans, especially urging those who lived close to the water to leave town.

The mayor announced that the Superdome would be ready to take people who could not evacuate. There was some talk about providing buses out of the city for those who had no transportation, but nothing was done.

"This is not a test," Nagin said. "We want you to take this a little more seriously and start moving."[2]

Interestingly enough, Amtrak—a nationwide passenger railroad company—offered to take evacuees out of New Orleans at no charge. City officials did not respond to the offer. By 8:30 P.M., the last train left the city. There were no passengers aboard. There was much confusion during this time, and communication between agencies was sorely lacking. In his defense, Nagin said that he never received the offer.

Twelve hours later, at 8:00 Sunday morning, the National Hurricane Center declared that Hurricane Katrina had become the strongest possible storm—a category 5. Experts said the storm would be devastating once it made landfall. Max Mayfield, director of the National Hurricane Center, called FEMA and warned them that the levees around New Orleans might be in big trouble. He told FEMA not to be surprised if the coastal surge would rise above the height of the levees.

FEMA stands for the Federal Emergency Management Agency. FEMA's role is to manage the federal response and recovery efforts before and after a natural disaster. If a governor declares a state of emergency because of a hurricane, tornado, flood, or other disaster, FEMA shows up. They bring food, water, and personnel, and they coordinate rescue organizations and shelters.

Even though he was reluctant to do so, Mayor Nagin announced a mandatory evacuation of New Orleans. "I wish I had better news," he said. "But we're facing the storm most of us have feared."[3] There were previous voluntary evacuations ordered, and it is very difficult for a local governing agency to force people to leave their own property. Thousands of people remained in their homes even after the "mandatory" evacuation.

Even President George W. Bush asked the people of New Orleans during a morning news conference to please evacuate the city. Still, people like William and Tena Corley decided to stay.

Finally, after what seemed like an excruciatingly long week waiting for the hurricane to strike, Katrina made landfall about 70 miles southeast of New

Orleans in a town called Buras, Louisiana, at 6:00 A.M. Monday, August 29. The hurricane arrived packing winds of 145 to 175 miles per hour.

For a moment there was a sigh of relief in New Orleans. Then the winds and the rains began to slam the Crescent City. The wind was whipping—tearing shingles from roofs and toppling trees—and the storm surge continued to rise. At about eight on Monday morning, the storm surge sent water spilling over the Industrial Canal. About an hour later, the 17th Street Canal ruptured. Located on the eastern side of the city, it suffered a 300-foot breach, allowing the waters of the Mississippi River to gush into the city's streets. The water destroyed many things in its path.

At about the same time, the devastating winds ripped off two large metal plates from the Louisiana Superdome, where 25,000 evacuees had sought shelter. Rainwater began to fall into the arena, causing an electrical outage. Backup generators were unable to power the entire building.

The storm shifted and started heading toward the Mississippi coast—but not before another levee, the London Avenue Canal on the northwest side of the city, failed as well. Water from the river was pouring into the city from this second spot. People started to panic. One report on National Public Radio said that at least 40,000 homes were flooded.

Before the storm left the city entirely, two remaining levees were breached. The water was rising, with no end in sight. Some news reports said the damage, if not the death toll, would be in the hundred thousands—as bad as the 2004 Asian tsunami.

Since some parts of the city remained dry, people started trying to return. They were enjoying the fact that it seemed New Orleans would be spared nature's fatal blow. Meanwhile, other areas of the city were under water, becoming part of nearby Lake Pontchartrain.

Officials with the Army Corps of Engineers went to inspect the levees. They told other government officials that another catastrophe was about to strike. They warned that floodwaters—200 feet wide—would sweep through the entire city over the next twenty-four hours. The danger was just beginning!

By Tuesday morning, four levees had been badly damaged. In all, there were fifty areas where water was coming through the levee system.

NEW ORLEANS AREA CANALS AND LEVEES

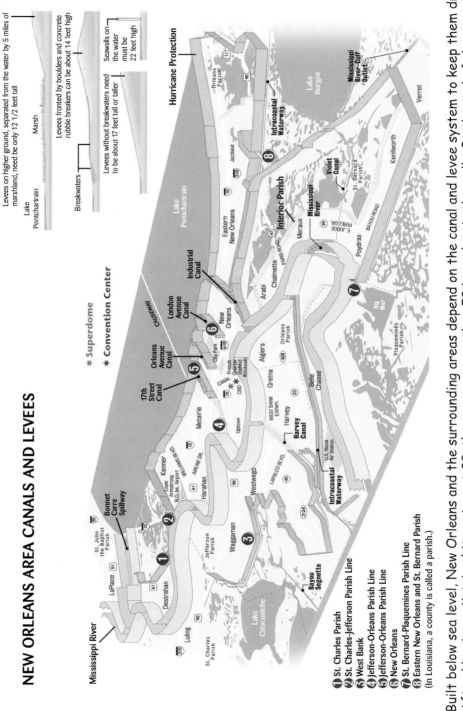

Levees on higher ground, separated from the water by 5 miles of marshland, need be only 12 1/2 feet tall

Lake Pontchartrain — Marsh

Levees fronted by boulders and concrete rubble breakers can be about 14 feet high

Seawalls on the water must be 22 feet high

Breakwaters

Levees without breakwaters need to be about 17 feet tall or taller

Hurricane Protection

Lake Pontchartrain

Superdome
Convention Center

Mississippi River

Bonnet Carre Spillway

17th Street Canal
Orleans Avenue Canal
London Avenue Canal
Industrial Canal
New Orleans

Metairie
Kenner
Louis Armstrong N.O. Int. Airport
Harahan
Waggaman
Westwego
Bayou Segnette
Lake Cataouatche
Luling
Destrehan
LaPlace
St. John the Baptist Parish
Jefferson Parish
St. Charles Parish

Uptown
City Park
CBD
French Quarter (behind Superdome)
Algiers
Gretna
Harvey
Belle Chasse
Harvey Canal
U.S. Naval Air Station
Intracoastal Waterway
WEST BANK EXPWY.
LAPALCO BLVD.

Orleans Parish
Arabi
Chalmette
Meraux
St. Bernard Parish
Violet Canal
Mississippi River
Interior Parish
Eastern New Orleans
Orleans Parish
Jazzland
E. JUDGE PEREZ DR.
BAYOU ROAD
Poydras
Big Mar
Plaquemines Parish
Kenilworth
Verret
Lake Borgne
Intracoastal Waterway
Mississippi River–Gulf Outlet
PARIS ROAD
CANAL

① St. Charles Parish
② St. Charles-Jefferson Parish Line
③ West Bank
④ Jefferson-Orleans Parish Line
⑤ Jefferson-Orleans Parish Line
⑥ New Orleans
⑦ St. Bernard-Plaquemines Parish Line
⑧ Eastern New Orleans and St. Bernard Parish

(In Louisiana, a county is called a parish.)

Built below sea level, New Orleans and the surrounding areas depend on the canal and levee system to keep them dry. After Hurricane Katrina hit on August 29, there were more than 50 breaches in the walls. By the end of the next day, 80 percent of the city was under water.

As all this was taking place, hundreds of people added more ugliness to the disaster. Even though no one had any idea yet whether people were dead or whether anyone needed rescuing, the city of New Orleans fell victim to lawlessness.

There were no police officers manning the streets. Storeowners had evacuated. National Guard troops had not yet arrived from the state capital or from other states that had promised help. People began breaking store windows and stealing. They looted food, clothes, televisions, computers—whatever they could walk away with.

They also started stealing guns.

Reports began coming in that nearly 100,000 innocent civilians living in a poor black neighborhood were trapped. They trudged through miles of waist-deep water to try to make it to the Superdome. They thought it would be safe there. They were wrong. There was only limited power. There was no air-conditioning and the toilets had stopped working. There were rumors that armed bandits were taking over the place.

Mayor Nagin ordered all of the city's police officers to try to establish some sort of order in the city. The city's newspaper, the *Times-Picayune,* reported on its web site that people were breaking in to pharmacies to steal medications and prescription drugs.

That the paper was still able to disseminate news is a testament to the staff's dedication. The Times-Picayune building was flooded in the hurricane, and many of the staffers' own homes were destroyed as well. Still, the reporters, editors, and photographers continued to cover the story. They worked out of a neighboring city's newsroom to get the news up on the paper's web site. By September 2, the paper was back in print.

When Governor Blanco visited the Superdome on August 30, she could not believe her eyes. She realized the situation there was desperate. She knew the dome needed to be evacuated, but there was no place for the people to go. The city was quickly going under water.

Angel Parker, who had sought shelter at the Superdome, said he did what he had to do to survive. Three days after leaving the Superdome and escaping to Baton Rouge, Parker said the conditions forced people to act in ways they did not want.

"It's just really bad because they had the technology to stop the levees from bursting," he said angrily outside the Pete Maravich Assembly Center at Louisiana State University—an emergency medical and food shelter. "The government wants to get mad at us but a lot of it is retaliation. You put all those people together and keep us caged up, I mean, c'mon, what did they expect?"[4]

As the situation deteriorated, it appeared as if no one was taking the lead, no one was in charge of relief or rescue efforts. The New Orleans Convention Center was opened, but no one knew whether there was enough food there for the evacuees. Army rescue helicopters also started dropping off rescued people at a spot on the interstate, expecting buses to pick them up and evacuate them from there. No one came for many days.

One of the most striking and macabre images from news coverage of the hurricane is that of ninety-one-year-old Booker Harris sitting in a lawn chair outside the convention center for two whole days after he died. There was nowhere to put the body. He was simply covered with a blanket. There were 20,000 people living at the convention center by this point, with no food, no organization, and very little hope that things would get better.

Back at the Superdome, trash and filth were piling higher and higher, clouding the area with a sickening stench. People were getting angry. They wanted to get out and leave, but no one came to help them. There was talk that women and children had been raped. There was no law.

The next morning, the two major hospitals in New Orleans ran out of gasoline for their emergency generators. No one knew what would happen to the critically ill patients who were too sick to be moved.

The city had become part of Lake Pontchartrain. The water in the streets was rising and falling with the tides. As National Guard troops began arriving, no one knew where to begin the rescue operations.

Meanwhile, Mississippi and Alabama, which had also been slammed by Katrina, were suffering devastating losses. Even though the actual damage caused by the hurricane was much worse in those areas, the people there were not in the same kind of danger as those in the city of New Orleans.

There was no power, no food, no sanitation, no law, and no rescue . . . yet.

FOR YOUR INFORMATION

Perhaps the government or the general public was slow to realize the panic and the devastation caused by Hurricane Katrina. However, there were many celebrities who were concerned about New Orleans, a city where scores of entertainers had made their mark.

Actor Sean Penn, who was in the area filming a movie about Louisiana politics, showed up at the Emergency Operations Center in Baton Rouge on September 3, offering whatever help he could. Turned away by federal and state emergency officials, Penn decided to take things into his own hands. He used his own money to obtain a boat, then toured the streets of New Orleans with a shotgun in his arms to try to find survivors.

Other stars helped as well, without going to such extremes as Sean Penn. Shortly after word of the hurricane and flooding hit the news, several celebrities held benefit concerts or made television appearances pleading for help from the American people. Guitarist Eric Clapton, singers Celine Dion and Harry Connick Jr., and comedian Bill Cosby were among the first to sign up for a special televised fundraising effort on CNN with famed television host Larry King.

While many, many singers lent their valuable voices to hurricane relief efforts, perhaps no one did more to help than New Orleans native Harry Connick Jr., the great jazz singer and musician. For Connick, his efforts and interests were also personal. His uncle John and his aunt Jessie had to be airlifted from the roof of their home. His band mates were also affected, with some of their homes being flooded and destroyed. But they were alive and safe. That inspired Connick to do more for others.

"It's a tragedy, it really is," he told *Today* show host Katie Couric about the situation. He also explained why some people were refusing to leave their homes even in the face of rising floodwaters. "People are afraid. They don't want to leave. They want to protect their homes . . . from looters."[5]

Harry Connick Jr. and Branford Marsalis perform the National Anthem at the New Orleans Saints home opener on September 19, 2005, at Giants Stadium in New Jersey.

Connick toured the city, calling conditions at some of the relief centers, including the Convention Center, despicable. Once they were evacuated, he said he was glad to see that there were no longer people staying in them.

Connick took part in relief efforts as well, even giving the shirt from his own back to an elderly man he found in a flooded home. Connick picked the man up and carried him out to safety.

Hurricane Katrina survivors scramble in waist-deep water outside the Superdome as a rescue helicopter approaches.

Thousands of people found themselves safe from the hurricane inside the Superdome, but tempers wore thin as resources began to run out.

CHAPTER 3

Rescue and Mayhem

Patrick LeBau saw a lot of violence and horrors when he was fighting for the U.S. Army in Iraq. He never thought he would have to witness again seeing someone killed before his eyes.

The United Sates went to war with Iraq in 2003 after President George W. Bush declared a war on terrorism. The federal government felt that Iraqi leader Saddam Hussein was an advocate of terrorism and dangerous to the United States.

When LeBau arrived home from Iraq in August, he hoped to go back to school, find a good job, and start his life. Then came Hurricane Katrina and all the violence and confusion that followed. LeBau had no idea he would see a virtual war zone materialize in his own country.

"I never saw anything like this before," he said, standing outside the Pete Maravich Assembly Center in Baton Rouge. "Baghdad has nothing on New Orleans. I never saw things like this in the war."[1]

LeBau went on to say that he saw a group of men beat an old man to death because he had whistled at a girl.

"Seeing that made me sick," he said. "We had to get out of there."[2]

LeBau and his family and friends—fourteen in all—fled the Superdome in New Orleans and somehow managed to make it to Baton Rouge, which is about 40 minutes away by car and was relatively untouched by Hurricane Katrina.

When they arrived, they found that the Baton Rouge shelters were full as well. They heard that a funeral parlor had stopped taking business and instead was using its space as an emergency shelter.

"We lost everything," said Gloria Peters, who was part of LeBau's group. "The water went right by our house and then came rushing right in. Can you believe we're staying at a funeral parlor?"[3]

As word of violence and mayhem in New Orleans spread, more and more evacuees fled the city and headed toward Baton Rouge or other cities.

"We have relatives in Texas," said Peters wearily. "We're going to try to make it to them and stay with them. I mean, we have nothing left. We have nothing."[4]

In New Orleans, lawlessness was widespread, hampering rescue efforts. The day before LeBau's group left the city, President Bush announced that the federal government was assisting in evacuating the Superdome, which had become unsafe. A few hours after the announcement, there were reports of gangs shooting at rescue helicopters that were trying to evacuate people from the Superdome. The situation was desperate.

National Guard troops were starting to show up, but no one really knew who was in charge. The Superdome had become a powder keg, and officials were worried that there would be widespread panic and death there. People were sitting in human waste. There was putrid, rotten garbage lying all over. People were hungry, thirsty, and hot.

"This is a national disgrace," said Terry Ebbert, who was in charge of emergency operations for New Orleans. "FEMA has been here for three days, yet there is no command and control. We can send massive amounts of aid to the tsunami victims [in Indonesia] but we can't bail out the city of New Orleans."[5]

Along with Mayor Nagin, Ebbert asked for buses to help evacuate the city. By this time, several people had died in the Superdome and at the Convention Center. Their images were plastered all over the nightly news, along with images of dead bodies floating through the city streets. The pictures on the news were so bad, and there was such little hope that things would quickly go back to normal, that many Americans became discouraged. Even the Speaker of the House of Representatives, Dennis Hastert, said that maybe New Orleans should just be abandoned. He said it may not make sense to rebuild the city.

Hope was dwindling as more and more reports of armed bandits circulated. Rescue workers arriving in the area were afraid to enter the city without

an escort. They were afraid the bandits would kill them and steal their emergency rescue supplies.

FEMA halted search and rescue operations because the city was too unsafe for emergency workers. Even Navy rescue operations were suspended for a short time because FEMA said it was unsafe to move within city streets.

Those who were helping out could also stay for only a short while. The sight and smell of dead bodies and the lawlessness were too much for many to handle. Counselors were brought in to assist.

"I don't have the words in my vocabulary to describe what is happening here," said Ozro Henderson, a medical team commander with FEMA. "Catastrophe and disaster don't explain it."[6]

Governor Blanco was fed up. The situation—especially regarding security and looting—had to change or else New Orleans would be lost forever. She said the city must be saved at all costs. She ordered the National Guard troops—who were armed with M-16 rifles—to shoot to kill if they saw looters or anyone else causing violence. This essentially made New Orleans a police state.

"There are some 40,000 extra troops that I have demanded," Blanco said. "They have M-16s and they're locked and loaded. . . . I have one message for these hoodlums: These troops know how to shoot and kill, and they are more than willing to do so if necessary, and I expect they will."[7]

Blanco was one of the first people to put a figure on the number of people killed by the hurricane. She estimated that thousands of people were dead.

Despite the mayhem and the finger-pointing that was going on all around the city and the country, there were massive rescue operations under way. Thousands of people were being found by emergency personnel and ushered to safety.

As a matter of fact, the military response to Hurricane Katrina was impressive. Just a day after the hurricane slammed the Gulf Coast region, military personnel and supplies began pouring into the area. Critics would say, however, that many of the soldiers sat around waiting for orders instead of conducting relief and rescue operations.

Four MH-53 and two HH-60 Pave Hawk helicopters from the assault ship *Bataan* began flying search-and-rescue missions almost immediately. Other Navy vessels joined the *Bataan* to provide support. U.S. military aircraft also flew in eight swift water boats that would be used to rescue people stranded

Looters take advantage of the disaster to rob merchandise from abandoned stores.

After stories of widespread looting were reported, National Guard soldiers who had been sent to protect New Orleans were ordered to stop looters—even if it meant shooting them.

in farmhouses. Three helicopters from Texas and five from Patrick Air Force Base in Florida were sent as well. The military predicted that before long there would be fifty or more helicopters on the scene to perform rescue operations.

That wasn't all. National Guard troops from more than twenty states were being sent to the region. Outside troops were necessary in part because of the U.S. war in Iraq. Roughly 3,000 National Guard troops from New Orleans and Mississippi were fighting overseas, so they were not available for the nation at home.

Pretty soon, evening newscasts were also showing and reporting stories of people waving at helicopters from their roofs and being whisked away to safety. Amid the devastation, there were finally glimmers of hope.

The team from Patrick Air Force Base specialized in search-and-rescue operations. In fact, the very unit that had performed numerous secret missions in Iraq and Afghanistan rescuing captured or fallen American soldiers was now being sent to the hurricane-ravaged area.

Finally, National Guard troops arrived at the Convention Center, bringing food and water to the hungry, dying people suffering in the heat. Their arrival caused most there to cheer and applaud. But then they started asking: "Where are the evacuation buses? When are we going to get out of here?"

Before long the *thwack-thwack-thwack* of helicopter blades filled the sky. Sometimes during the day, up to twenty helicopters could be spotted in the sky at the same time. Copters were swooping down on homes where people waved from rooftops just a few feet above water.

Despite the rescues, people were still dazed and scared of the future.

"Some guys with guns showed up one night and harassed us," said Lisa Mansion of New Orleans. "Then last night we got picked up by the helicopter and brought here. Now, we have no idea where we're going. Can you imagine living in one place your whole life and not knowing where you're going?"[8]

Nonmilitary and nonemergency personnel also began helping out. Commercial airlines like American, Continental, JetBlue, Delta, and others

With water levels reaching more than ten feet high, many people who had chosen not to evacuate climbed up to their roofs, where they felt safest. They also hoped that rescue helicopters would see them there.

People on a New Orleans rooftop ask soldiers in a helicopter for help.

Civilians form a line to help unload ready-to-eat meals and water.

Outstanding effort was made by civilians, military personnel, and emergency workers to help the victims of the hurricane.

donated their airplanes to be used for evacuation efforts at New Orleans International Airport.

One interesting tale involved Master Sergeant Omar Rivera. He was allowed to leave the Patrick Air Force Base in Melbourne, Florida, for a couple of days to deliver generators to his family. They lived in south Florida and had lost power when Hurricane Katrina whisked over the Keys.

As soon as he came back to the base, Rivera—a forty-three-year-old flight engineer—joined thirty-seven of his comrades on rescue missions in New Orleans and Mississippi. Flying helicopters in flooded residential areas with downed power lines is a dangerous undertaking, but Rivera said they would exercise caution and just go where ordered. This highly recognizable unit is known as the 920th Rescue Wing.

"It all depends where they send us," Rivera said. "We'll go to Mississippi first. It could be anywhere that we go."[9]

So, clad in their olive green flight suits, they took off for New Orleans and Mississippi with one goal in mind: to save lives.

FOR YOUR INFORMATION

Despite differences in politics with other nations, the United States often leads the way in responding with help when there is a disaster somewhere in the world. Just in 2005, the U.S. pledged millions and millions of dollars in aid and military support for victims of the Asian tsunami, as well as for those of catastrophic mudslides in Central America and of a killer earthquake in Pakistan.

When Hurricane Katrina laid waste to New Orleans, the world responded in kind.

Almost immediately there were offers pouring in from other countries promising money, equipment, soldiers, planes, and specialists. In all, more than fifty countries around the globe pledged assistance. The Australian government immediately sent $7.7 million to the American Red Cross and also sent along a team of emergency management experts to help coordinate efforts.

Chandrika Kumaratunga

"The United States is so often at the forefront of international aid efforts to help less fortunate nations," said Australian Foreign Minister Alexander Downer.[10]

England and Germany also promised help. France offered several aircraft and a special disaster unit with twenty soldiers. But maybe the most touching pledge of aid came from the tiny nation of Sri Lanka, which suffered devastating losses during the December 2004 tsunami.

"Having experienced the fury of nature ourselves during the tsunami, the people of Sri Lanka and I fully empathize with you at this hour of national grief,"[11] said Sri Lankan President Chandrika Kumaratunga. She pledged $25,000 to the American Red Cross.

U.S. Secretary of State Condoleezza Rice said it was important to accept the aid that was offered, especially from the poorer countries. "It is very valuable for people to be able to give to each other and to be able to do so without a sense of means,"[12] she said. She also announced aid offers from Cuba and Venezuela, two countries with very strained relationships with the United States.

Condoleezza Rice

Tears well in the eyes of Bruce Gordon, President of the NAACP, when he sees the conditions inside the Riverside Center in Baton Rouge, Louisiana.

Organizations like the NAACP visited shelters to see whether the evacuees were being treated well. Gordon criticized some government officials for calling the evacuated citizens "refugees."

CHAPTER 4

Tensions Mount

As rescue efforts and evacuations plodded slowly along in the days after Hurricane Katrina slammed the Gulf Coast, it became evident that the people most affected in New Orleans were those in the black community. Many of these people were just too poor to evacuate, and many had nowhere to go. As television images showed them being evacuated, the media and government officials referred to them as refugees. This term usually refers to people fleeing foreign countries to avoid violence, war, or oppression. The comparison became a rallying point for people in the black community, many of whom already felt disconnected from mainstream society. They were insulted by the term *refugee*. The black community and many others came to believe that relief efforts and the government's response would have been quicker if most of the people affected had been white and not black.

It seemed as if the country had moved back in time forty years, when race relations were very tense during the civil rights movement. There was danger that violence might erupt if help did not arrive soon, especially for the black community. There were accusations of racism.

Bruce Gordon, the president of the National Association for the Advancement of Colored People (NAACP), flew to Louisiana to survey the damage and see whether the black community was being served or shortchanged. His first stop was at the Baton Rouge Riverside Center, a relief shelter where many black people from New Orleans who had no place else to go were staying. Several people complained to him that conditions inside the shelter were terrible. They said there wasn't enough security and that evacuees were not able to come and go freely from the building.

When Gordon walked in and saw the thousands of people lying on cots and on the ground looking lost and afraid, he started to cry. Finally, after com-

posing himself, he grabbed the microphone and addressed the people: "I want you to know that you are not alone," he said, choking back tears. "We don't see you as refugees. We see you as American citizens."[1]

One of the evacuees who spoke to Gordon was Ronald Evans from New Orleans. He was fed up with the government's response and was thinking of moving his wife and little daughter to his van parked outside.

"It's horrible. We're ready just to live in the streets," he said, his eyes laced with desperation. "The officers talk badly to us and treat us like criminals. Where is the government help? I really believe the government would have responded quicker if we were white."[2]

Gordon found the officers in charge and complained, but little would change. "These people are almost imprisoned," he said. "They are being treated like convicts. I think the government can do more. We seem to have become refugees, a term we all despise. We are American citizens who have become displaced. There are more resources. We need to save ourselves."[3]

One night earlier, singer Kanye West stunned the nation by announcing on national television during a fund-raising concert that President George W. Bush did not care about black people. "I hate the way they treat us in the media," he said. "When you see a black family it says they're looting. When you see a white family, they're looking for food. . . . George Bush doesn't care about black people."[4]

But Darrell Glasper of the Baton Rouge NAACP refused to call the problems a black and white issue. He said the problems ran much deeper than mere color. "It's a class thing. It's not black and white," he said. "It was only poor people who couldn't get out of New Orleans in time. We are talking about the lower totem pole in class. Even the people who had cars couldn't get to them. There was a rush of water, man."[5] Glasper was referring to people who chose not to leave the city until the levees had burst and the streets were flooded. Many cars were ruined or simply inaccessible because of the water.

Former Secretary of State Colin Powell agreed. He said that only 10 percent of the people in poor New Orleans neighborhoods had cars, and that hardly any of them had a credit card.

Loads of people who were lucky enough to be taken out of the city by military helicopters were dropped off on Interstate 110. In some cases they were left there for days with no shelter, waiting for help to come.

One of those, Lamar Robinson, was there for a while with his elderly mother when he saw that she had stopped breathing. He screamed for paramedics or for anyone to come help. Finally, some paramedics responded and resuscitated her. A helicopter arrived moments later and took her to a mobile hospital unit. It looked as though she had been saved in time.

"Our home was flooded with ten feet of water," Robinson said, crying. "We were there for a few days on the roof. I just want my mother to live."[6]

Tensions were also high among emergency personnel and rescue workers as there continued to be confusion regarding evacuation and rescue efforts. Two charity hospitals in New Orleans were not fully evacuated until Friday, September 2, four full days after the hurricane was gone.

With no food, power, or water, hospital staffers who stayed behind to save the critically ill fed themselves intravenously so that they would not dehydrate. The hospitals were flooded, the morgues were full, and corpses floated through the hospital hallways.

Dr. Fred Cerise, an official with the Louisiana Department of Health and Hospitals, shook his head. He could not believe how rescuers had taken healthy people out before coming for those who needed urgent medical care from the hospital. Even though there had been a mandatory evacuation, many hospital patients had been too sick or fragile to move. Now they needed rescuing, too.

A day later, Dr. Ryan Bird was walking aimlessly through the water-filled streets of New Orleans outside Charity Hospital, which is part of the LSU Medical Center in New Orleans. He had not shaved since the storm hit, and he looked lost. He had just spent the day removing dead bodies from the hospital.

"It's just chaos," he said slowly. "Nobody is working together. There are a lot of people here to help but nobody knows what to do."[7]

When asked how he was dealing with seeing all the dead bodies, Dr. Bird said that there would be thousands more to deal with once the water receded and the levees were repaired. "You just learn to put up a wall," he said, before turning to walk back into the hospital to continue the gruesome task.[8]

There were also tensions between New Orleans rescue personnel and National Guard troops. The City of New Orleans Deputy Police Commander W. S. Riley criticized the federal government's effort. "The Guard arrived 48 hours after the hurricane with 40 trucks. They drove their trucks in and went to sleep," he said. "For 72 hours the police department and fire department

and a handful of citizens were alone in rescuing people. We have people who died while the National Guard sat and played cards. I understand why we are not winning the war in Iraq if this is what we have."[9]

Many of the evacuees who did make it out of New Orleans decided to go to Texas. In Houston there was an empty baseball stadium, the Astrodome. Buses were leaving Louisiana filled with evacuees heading for Houston.

By Saturday, September 3, the last of the evacuees were removed from the Superdome and from the city's Convention Center. The Big Easy was now a ghost town, left to the dead and dying. The only evidence of life were the occasional stragglers, like William and Tena Corley or the young National Guard soldiers patrolling city corners with loaded M-16s.

Cars were overturned. Buildings and storefronts had been broken into and gutted. Anything worth stealing had long been taken. Garbage and waste combined with the sickening smell of dead and decaying bodies, filling the air with an unforgettable stench.

"No one knows how many were killed by Hurricane Katrina's floods and how many more succumbed waiting to be rescued. But the bodies are everywhere: hidden in attics, floating among the ruined city, crumpled on wheelchairs, abandoned on highways," reported Allen Breed. "The dying goes on."[10]

During this time, political strategies may have led to a slower response or a less organized one than could have been achieved. President Bush asked Governor Blanco to sign papers that would let the federal government take over all the National Guard activities in New Orleans and the rest of the state. It would unite the rescuers, instead of having so many independent units acting without knowing what the others were doing. Blanco knew that for her Democratic party, signing would be seen as a weakness.

Bush on the other hand could have taken over the state by instituting the Insurrection Act, a law that would put the federal government in charge of the state of Louisiana. But then he worried about how it would look for a male Republican president to take power away from a female Democratic governor.

During this time President Bush also made several trips to the New Orleans area to survey the damage and see how rescue operations were going. While it gave some people comfort to see that the President cared about the area, most people were wondering when New Orleans would once again be above water.

While thousands of New Orleans residents made their way to Houston and other parts of Texas, it seemed as if Mother Nature had it in for them. Another massive hurricane, this one dubbed Rita, had its sights set squarely on the Lone Star State.

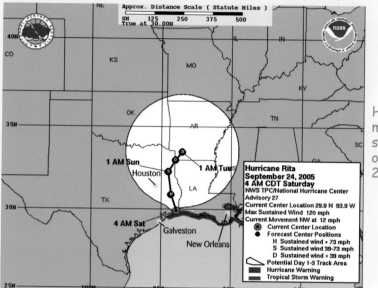

Hurricane Rita made landfall in southeast Texas on September 24, 2005.

The storm was so dangerous that more than a million people in its path evacuated. The National Weather Service called it the third most intense storm in history.

Max Mayfield, director of the National Hurricane Center, warned people not to take the storm lightly. He predicted it could be even more damaging than Katrina. While projections had the storm hitting the Galveston, Texas, area, there were fears that it could veer east and slam New Orleans again, demolishing the crippled city.

Evacuees who had made it to Texas did not know what to do or where to go next.

Gwendolyn Garley, who was rescued with her family from their roof in New Orleans, said she had wanted to settle in Galveston permanently.

"I feel lifeless, I'm just going through the motions," she said.[11]

The hurricane slowed in the Gulf of Mexico, causing a storm surge that damaged the repaired levees in New Orleans. The breaches reopened and parts of New Orleans were flooded once more. Whole towns along the Louisiana coast were demolished.

Then, instead of gaining strength and causing the devastation everyone feared, the storm weakened slightly and made landfall in southeast Texas in very rural areas. The storm surge expected in Galveston and the heavy rains in New Orleans never came, making it easier to repair the levees once again.

Even though it seemed as if the country had dodged a bullet, Rita still claimed about 10 lives, caused two million residences to loose their electricity, and racked up more than $9 billion in damage.

A Chinook helicopter drops sandbags into the rushing water of a levee that was demolished by Hurricane Katrina.

In addition to searching for survivors of the hurricane, the U.S. armed forces were involved in repairing the damaged levees. Bags were filled with rocks and sand, then placed in the breaches to slow down the water flow.

Drying Out and Moving Back

Despite the deaths, the flooding, and the mandatory evacuations, there were still people in New Orleans who refused to leave. The city's mayor, as well as many emergency officials, felt the city should be completely empty so that repairs could be made and sanitary measures taken.

Experts and doctors with the Centers for Disease Control and Prevention tested the water that was in the city's streets and announced that it had more than ten times the allowable sewage-related bacteria. They warned people not to touch the water, because they could get very sick or die.

Mayor Nagin ordered a forced evacuation. Police officers and National Guard soldiers had to spend several days going door to door throughout the entire city. Incredibly, they found more than 10,000 people who had refused to leave. These people were given no more choice. New Orleans was unsafe. They had to leave. They were put into boats and helicopters and whisked away.

After the city of New Orleans was successfully evacuated, engineers went hard to work at fixing the levees that had burst and flooded the city.

Thousands of sandbags filled with sand and rocks, weighing 300 pounds apiece, were used to keep the water from continuing to flow in from the city's 17th Street Canal. Once the canal was patched, the engineers were able to repair water pumps and start pumping water out of the city. The Army Corps of Engineers patched up the breach in the London Avenue Canal as well. Soon the city would no longer be under water.

As water dried and more and more bodies were being discovered in the streets, the government banned media from entering the city and photographing the damage or the dead. NBC reporter Brian Williams even said that he and his film crew were prevented from filming by National Guard soldiers holding them at gunpoint.

Mayor Ray Nagin ordered a forced evacuation of New Orleans because of dangerously high levels of bacteria in the city's floodwaters.

Police officers and other rescue crews acting on his order found an incredible 10,000 people still in the city. Like many other officials, Nagin was unhappy with the federal government's response time in coming to his city's aid.

The federal government was clearly embarrassed that recovery efforts seemed to go very slowly in the days after the hurricane. It admitted that perhaps more people would have been saved if response had been quicker.

The U.S. Congress approved nearly $60 billion in aid for hurricane relief, but the government was still coming under fire for the slow response. People—including New York Senator Hillary Rodham Clinton—called for FEMA director Michael Brown to resign.

President Bush did not fire Brown, but he did replace him regarding Hurricane Katrina relief efforts with Coast Guard officer Vice Admiral Thad Allen. Bush then took some of the responsibility for the slow response. Brown would later be replaced as the head of FEMA.

"How many people died as a result of us not having the resources to get people water, to get them pulled out of harm's way quick enough to get them evacuated out of the city?"[1] Nagin asked.

While the country and the government officials involved were playing the "blame game," stories began to emerge of true heroism, people who went way

above and beyond the call of duty to save human lives. Their stories are truly inspiring.

One of those heroes, Dan Culberson, spent five straight days flying a Chinook helicopter trying to save lives. The Army Chief Warrant Officer is credited with saving an incredible 839 people.

For those five days, Culberson stopped only to eat quick meals and to refuel his helicopter, which could fit 30 evacuees at a time.

"They were so grateful," he said. "Many of them were slapping high-fives to crew members and it was just joy."[2]

Culberson said it was the best assignment he had ever been on with the army. What he liked most, he said, was that he had a chance to save American lives.

Another incredible story of heroism was sixty-two-year-old Vivian Delaney of New Orleans. She was trapped with her elderly mother inside her mother's house. After a few days there was no food or water left. There was no power, and even the toilets had stopped working. Her mother became limp and her eyes starting looking weaker and weaker. She needed food desperately.

Delaney waved frantically at helicopters that were whizzing by and circling overhead in search of hurricane victims who needed saving. Because their house was hidden by trees, they were not spotted.

Delaney's own house was a few city streets away. Even though she couldn't swim, she knew that she couldn't let her mother die in front of her.

"My mother's lips were so dry," she would later say from a hospital. "I couldn't just let her die. So I prayed to God to help me and guide me."[3]

Delaney took a few steps into the water and plummeted straight down. It was over her head. She reached her arms up, not knowing what else to do. Her life was leaving her body as the air was going out of her lungs.

Suddenly, she felt a hand reach down into the warm water and pull her up. The rescue worker dragged her to safety, and then also rescued Delaney's mother. It was a miracle! Delaney never did find out the name of her hero.[4]

Other heroes were Florida missionary Joe Hurston and his family. Hurston, who deploys portable water purifiers to areas where natural disasters have contaminated fresh water supplies, was one of the first on the scene with his water machines in Banda Aceh, Indonesia, days after the Asian tsunami killed thousands of people in late December 2004.

Then in July 2005, something in his local newspaper caught his eye. It was a little blurb about how the Indian city of Bombay had suffered the worst rains in recorded history. A few thousand people were reported to be killed in the flooding. There were floods everywhere. The city of 11 million people had no sanitation system, and the water there was polluted. The heavy rains and dead bodies would only make clean water harder to find. Hurston quickly deployed and was soon on a plane with his wife, daughter, and a family friend.

One week into his mission, Hurston saw that Hurricane Katrina was headed straight for New Orleans and Louisiana. He left his wife and friend behind to finish helping in India and headed straight home for Florida.

"I'm from Louisiana," he said. "That's my home. I had to go and take care of my people."[5]

Hurston didn't waste any time. He called in all the favors that people owed him, and before long he had lined up a fleet of six small airplanes. With the smallest crew necessary, Hurston deployed sixty water purifiers to his hometown of Baton Rouge.

He attended government and relief organization meetings and urged them to let him get to areas in downtown New Orleans that were most affected. There were some concerns, however. There were reports of armed gangs taking over the city. Hurston didn't care. He spent the next ten days traveling through the Gulf Coast states, bringing the gift of fresh water.

Another group of people traveled all the way from Honolulu, Hawaii, to become heroes, though they never intended to be. They were four women paramedics who thought it would be a lot of fun to save their money and vacation time to attend a conference on new paramedic techniques. The conference was in New Orleans.

They arrived just before Hurricane Katrina struck. They were safe but stranded in their hotel room, which was located in the city's historic French Quarter. After a few days, the hotel was out of food and water. The women would have to evacuate to the city's convention center.

Along the way, they carried an elderly man with a broken leg and gave first aid to injured people. Once they arrived at the convention center, the four Hawaiians gave first aid and comfort to hundreds of injured evacuees. When they were finished, they refused to rest. They went to work on the police offic-

ers who were suffering from rashes, exhaustion, and dehydration. When they arrived home in Hawaii, the four were greeted by throngs of people as heroes.

There was also the story of Daisy, a seventy-pound dog left behind by her owners with enough food for days. They thought they would be back before the food ran out. More than a month after the hurricane, the dog—who miraculously lived—was reunited with her family, who had moved to Ohio. They were overjoyed to see that their pet had survived.

Heroes, death, blame, politics, Hurricane Katrina, and New Orleans will be in the news for years to come as people unravel exactly what happened and figure out how to keep it from ever happening again. At least 1,400 people were killed by the hurricane in Louisiana and Mississippi. Thousands more were missing. Damages reached $130 billion.

By February 2006, tens of thousands of people who had been displaced by the hurricane were still homeless. Many were living in hotel rooms, but FEMA was ending its hotel subsidy program. FEMA officials claimed that people should be applying for long-term housing assistance, even if they had to move permanently to new states.[6] That wouldn't be easy for people who had lost everything.

Despite the finger-pointing and the devastation to the area, there was still hope that New Orleans would once again rise to be the Crescent City, the Big Easy, the hub of jazz music that it once was.

In a televised address to the nation on September 15, 2005, from an empty New Orleans, President Bush promised just that.

"These days of sorrow and outrage have also been marked by acts of courage and kindness that make all Americans proud," he said. "We will do what it takes, we will stay as long as it takes, to help citizens rebuild their communities and their lives. And all who question the future of the Crescent City need to know there is no way to imagine America without New Orleans, and this great city will rise again."[7]

The President followed up on that promise by pledging $3.1 billion to the city to bolster the levee system. At least half of that money would be used for a state-of-the-art pumping system that would allow the city to close three canals.

"It's important that people feel safe and move back into the area," Bush said. "The levee system will be better and stronger than it ever has been in the history of New Orleans."[8]

By February 2006, fish were once again swimming in the aquarium instead of city streets, children were back in school, businesses were up and running, the National Football League promised to help rebuild the Superdome, and life was returning to normal.

Then, incredibly enough, on February 2, several tornadoes ripped through some of the New Orleans neighborhoods that were still struggling to make a comeback from the 2005 hurricane season. Many houses lost roofs in the tornadoes, and the airport suffered damage as well. At least no one was hurt.

It may take years for New Orleans to recover from the deadly hurricane, which killed at least 1,417 people. It may also take years for the country to figure out what went wrong with rescue efforts and why victims weren't helped sooner.

Hearings were held in the nation's capital to try to figure out what went wrong. President Bush acknowledged that the response "at every level of government was not well coordinated and was overwhelmed in the first few days."[9] He added, "Americans have every right to expect a more effective response in a time of emergency."[10]

As policymakers were looking at the past, some began running straight into the future. Louisiana Governor Kathleen Blanco formed what she called a Dream Team of urban planners, architects, and builders to put their heads together and figure out the best way to rebuild New Orleans.

President George W. Bush and Governor Kathleen Blanco

Meanwhile thousands of the people could not move back into their homes, and some had returned to find dead relatives under the rubble. By mid-January 2006, there were still 3,200 people missing. Many survivors will never recover emotionally or financially from the killer storm, and the nation's politics will likely suffer for a while as well.

In the end, as President Bush said, an act of nature can be difficult to deal with, but it is important to be resilient and not give up.

"In the life of this nation, we have often been reminded that nature is an awesome force, and that all life is fragile. . . . Americans have never left our destiny to the whims of nature and we will not start now," he said.[11]

Chronology

August 23, 2005	National Hurricane Center recognizes a weather disturbance that will become Hurricane Katrina
August 26	The hurricane reaches category 2 status
August 27	Katrina becomes a "major hurricane"
August 28	The Superdome opens for evacuees; Mayor Ray Nagin orders a mandatory evacuation of New Orleans; not everyone leaves
August 29	6:00 A.M. Hurricane Katrina makes landfall in Buras, Louisiana, 70 miles southeast of New Orleans
	8:00 A.M. Storm surge crests over Industrial Canal
	9:00 A.M. 17th Street levee ruptures; parts of Superdome roof are torn off
	London Avenue Canal fails
	Looting begins
August 30	Louisiana National Guardsmen deployed; search and rescue operations continue, with 350 boats in the water and two helicopter squadrons flying overhead; hospital evacuation begins; Ernest N. Morial Convention Center is open for evacuees, but it is not stocked with food and water; 80 percent of the city is under water by the end of the day
August 31	Additional National Guardsmen are deployed; Governor Blanco calls for total evacuation of the city; Superdome evacuation begins, and people are bused to Houston
September 1	More National Guardsmen are deployed; rescue helicopters are fired upon as they try to evacuate the Superdome
September 2	President Bush visits New Orleans
September 5	A forced evacuation of the city is under way
September 15	President Bush promises that New Orleans will be rebuilt and rise again
September 21	New Orleans residents re-evacuate ahead of Hurricane Rita
September 22	A storm surge caused by Hurricane Rita causes repaired levee breaches to rupture, and parts of New Orleans flood again
October 10	Louisiana police say they are able to identify only 200 of the 1,000 dead bodies found to date
October 24	Hurricane Wilma, the most intense hurricane ever recorded in the Atlantic, causes severe damage in southwestern Florida
November 30	The record hurricane season, which produced seven major hurricanes, officially ends
December 1	FEMA promises to have all evacuees in permanent housing but misses the deadline
December 21	The National Hurricane Center says that Hurricane Katrina was actually a category 3 storm
January 2, 2006	The aquarium restocks many of the animals it lost during the hurricane
January 31	The National Football League votes to help the New Orleans Saints rebuild the Superdome
February 7	Thousands are still in need of permanent housing; FEMA begins phasing out the last of the hotel subsidies
February 17	Convention Center reopens for business

Further Reading

Books

Editors of Time Magazine, *Time: Hurricane Katrina: The Storm That Changed America* (Alexandria, Virginia: Time, 2005).

Moyer, Susan M. *Hurricane Katrina: Stories of Rescue, Recovery and Rebuilding in the Eye of the Storm* (Champaign, Illinois: Spotlight Press LLC, 2005).

On the Internet

FEMA for Kids
http://www.fema.gov/kids/

Images of Hurricane Rita and Hurricane Katrina
http://www.ritaimages.com/

National Weather Service National Hurricane Center
http://www.nhc.noaa.gov/

Right Wing Nut House
Katrina: Response Timeline
http://rightwingnuthouse.com/archives/2005/09/04/katrina-response-timeline/

Chapter Notes

Chapter 1 Honeymoon in New Orleans

1. Personal interview with Tena and William Corley, New Orleans, September 3, 2005.

2. Ibid.

3. Ibid.

4. Ibid.

5. Ibid.

Chapter 2 Surprise Storm?

1. Farhad Manjoo, Page Rockwell, and Aaron Kinney, "Timeline to Disaster," Salon.com, September 15, 2005, http://www.salon.com/news/feature/2005/09/15/katrina_timeline/index_np.html

2. Ibid.

3. Ibid.

4. Personal interview with Angel Parker at Louisiana State University in Baton Rouge, September 2, 2005.

5. Interview on the *Today* show with Katie Couric, September 6, 2005.

Chapter 3 Rescue and Mayhem

1. Personal interview with Patrick LeBau at Louisiana State University in Baton Rouge, September 2, 2005.

2. Ibid.

3. Personal interview with Gloria Peters at Louisiana State University in Baton Rouge, September 2, 2005.

4. Ibid.

5. Associated Press, September 1, 2005; as reported by Josh White and Peter Whoriskey in "Planning, Response Are Faulted," *Washington Post*, Friday, September 2, 2005, p. A01.

6. CNN.com, "Military Due to Move in to New Orleans," September 2, 2005.

7. Ibid.

Chapter Notes

8. Sandy Davis and Jessica Fender, "Evacuees Recount Ordeal Waiting for Help to Arrive," *The Advocate,* September 3, 2005, p. 10A.

9. Juan Ortega, "Local Unit Will Assist in Rescue," *Florida Today,* August 31, 2005, p. 7A.

10. Barry Schweid, AP Diplomatic Writer, "Aid Pours In from Around Globe," *The Advocate,* September 3, 2005, p. 10A.

11. CNN.com, "World Leaders Offer Sympathy, Aid," September 2, 2005.

12. Schweid.

Chapter 4 Tensions Mount

1. Personal observation, Baton Rouge Riverside Center, September 3, 2005.

2. Personal interview with Ronald Evans at Baton Rouge Riverside Center, September 3, 2005.

3. Personal observation, Baton Rouge Riverside Center, September 3, 2005.

4. "A Concert for Hurricane Relief," NBC, September 2, 2005.

5. Personal interview with Darrell Glasper at NAACP headquarters in Baton Rouge, September 2, 2005.

6. Sandy Davis and Jessica Fender, "Evacuees Recount Ordeal Waiting for Help to Arrive," *The Advocate,* September 3, 2005, p. 1A.

7. Personal interview with Dr. Ryan Bird, New Orleans, September 3, 2005.

8. Ibid.

9. Farhad Manjoo, Page Rockwell, and Aaron Kinney, "Timeline to Disaster," Salon.com, September 15, 2005.

10. Allen Breed, "Dead Uncounted" *Mobile Register,* September 4, 2005, p. 1A.

11. CNN.com, "Texans Flee Colossal Rita," September 21, 2005, http://www.cnn.com/2005/WEATHER/09/21/rita/

Chapter 5 Drying Out and Moving Back

1. Knight Ridder, Washington Bureau, "Government's Failures Doomed Many in Katrina's Path," September 11, 2005.

2. Gannett News Service Special Report: "Katrina Heroes."

3. Sandy Davis and Jessica Fender, "Evacuees Recount Ordeal Waiting for Help to Arrive," *The Advocate,* September 3, 2005, p. 10A.

4. Ibid.

5. Personal interview with Joe Hurston on a twin engine plane flying to Baton Rouge, September 2, 2005.

6. Michelle Goldberg, "Homeless Again in New Orleans," Salon.com, February 7, 2006, http://www.salon.com/news/feature/2006/02/07/hotels/index_np.html

7. "Transcript: Bush Katrina Address," September 15, 2005, http://www.foxnews.com/story/0,2933,169514,00.html

8. CNN.com, "Levee Plan Prompts Call to 'Come Home,'" December 15, 2005, http://www.cnn.com/2005/POLITICS/12/15/bush.levees/?section=cnn_space

9. Jim VandeHei and Peter Baker, "Bush Pledges Historic Effort To Help Gulf Coast Recover; President Says U.S. Will Learn From Mistakes," September 16, 2005, p. A01.

10. Ibid.

11. "Transcript: Bush Katrina Address."

Glossary

bacteria (bak-TEE-ree-ah)
Microorganisms of various forms that often cause sickness and disease.

civil rights movement
The struggles between 1955 and 1968 to end racial discrimination in the United States.

evacuation (ee-vaa-kyoo-AY-shun)
The departing of large numbers of people from a dangerous place.

evacuee (ee-VAA-kyoo-EE)
A person who leaves a dangerous place.

landfall
Reaching land, usually from the sea.

levee (LEH-vee)
A built-up embankment meant to keep a body of water from overflowing.

police state
An area controlled by police who enforce laws without using regular legal procedures.

racism (RAY-sih-zum)
Reacting to a person or people solely on the basis of their race.

refugee (reh-fyoo-JEE)
One who flees to one country to escape danger and seeks protection in another.

Saffir-Simpson Hurricane Scale (SAA-feer SIMP-son)
A 1 to 5 rating system for measuring hurricane intensity.

tsunami (sue-NAH-mee)
A huge ocean wave caused by an underwater earthquake.

vermin (VER-min)
Potentially harmful animals that are difficult to control.

Author's Note

I had always wanted to visit the Big Easy—the Crescent City of New Orleans. Living fairly close by in Florida, I knew I'd make it there someday, perhaps to revel in Mardi Gras or catch the latest jazz sounds in some smoky club or just to tour the historic areas and the French Quarter. I regret that it took Hurricane Katrina to bring me to New Orleans.

Having experienced a slew of hurricanes these last few years in Florida and having traveled to Asia a few days after the killer tsunami of 2004, I had already seen my share of natural disasters and the devastating

John A. Torres (left) and Joe Hurston

toll they can take in the form of lives lost, property damaged, and hope vanquished.

My friend Joe Hurston (see page 39) called me Friday morning, September 2, 2005, and told me he was leaving that night for Baton Rouge. He wanted to help with relief efforts. I asked him if he had room for me on the tiny twin engine plane, and a few hours later we landed in Louisiana.

After pulling some strings and calling in some favors, we were able to secure passes from FEMA that would get us into downtown New Orleans the following morning. I saw tons of volunteers, convoys of military vehicles, and skies filled with helicopters.

Yet, when I finally set foot in the Big Easy, I expected to see relief, gratitude, and of course sadness. Instead I saw a lot of mixed emotions and a lot of anger. I met people who refused to speak with me because the media had been referring to them as refugees. I met people who said that "white" America did not care about "black" America.

I asked one man if he wanted a bottle of water and he looked at me with disdain. "Do I look dehydrated to you?" he asked, before turning and walking away.

I walked through shelters in Baton Rouge where evacuees wearing Nike sneakers and designer clothes criticized the federal government and lamented that the poor in this country are often forgotten.

I felt like an intruder, an outsider in my own country.

I couldn't help thinking of the people I had met in Indonesia: the woman who thanked me for helping out after the tsunami killed four of her children; the hordes of children who cheered and greeted us with smiles when we gave them clean water, even though their homes had been reduced to rubble. I remember the man who was still looking for his daughter, ten days after she had been swept away by the ocean, and how he offered me the spare room in his home.

Of course there were also people like Tena and William Corley, who stopped their scramble for supplies to tell me this story and to ask for prayers. They also wanted to thank the rest of the country for not forgetting about them.

I left New Orleans thinking about how lucky Americans are. We are lucky to live in a place where the poor can wear Nike sneakers and have cable television. We are lucky that we really don't know what poor is. It was an important lesson I learned and helped prepare me for a trip to Bombay, India, in October—home to Asia's largest shantytown slum where children are trained from a very young age to beg in the streets.

I still plan to go back to the Big Easy one of these days. I still want to listen to jazz and enjoy the Mardi Gras madness, and I still want to get to know the real people of New Orleans—when things calm down a little bit.

—February 2006

Index